Investment Guide for the Stock Market

C. P. Kumar
Reiki Healer
Roorkee - 247667, India

Disclaimer

While every effort has been made to ensure the accuracy and completeness of the content in this book, the author cannot guarantee that the information contained herein is error-free, up-to-date, or suitable for every individual circumstance.

The author shall not be held liable or responsible for any errors or omissions in the content of the book, nor for any damages, or losses that may arise from any actions taken based upon the suggestions or contents presented in the book.

Readers are advised to use their own judgment and discretion in applying the information provided in this book, and to consult with qualified professionals before taking any action based on the contents of this book. The author disclaims any and all liability or responsibility for any actions taken or not taken based on the information contained in this book.

DEDICATION

To the dreamers, the believers, and the steadfast seekers of financial wisdom,

This book is dedicated to you – the individuals who aspire to navigate the intricate tapestry of the stock market with prudence and purpose. As you embark on this journey of investment in pursuit of your financial goals, I am honored to share in your pursuit of knowledge and understanding.

Each chapter of this book is a thread carefully woven into the fabric of your investment acumen. From the very foundation of understanding the stock market's intricate mechanics to the heights of deciphering market trends and cycles, you have shown the courage to embrace complexity.

To those who grasp the difference between investment and speculation, who appreciate the orchestra of market indices conducting the rhythm of economic growth, and who identify the delicate balance between risk and reward, I commend your dedication to becoming informed investors.

As you dive into the seas of fundamental and technical analysis, traversing the terrains of value and growth investing, remember that knowledge is your compass. Your navigation through the tempestuous waters of human psychology and behavioral biases demonstrates your commitment to understanding the facets of emotional intelligence.

Just as a skilled painter blends colors on a canvas, your mastery of diversification strategies and asset allocation creates a masterpiece of a well-balanced portfolio. The art of portfolio rebalancing echoes your dedication to maintaining equilibrium in the pursuit of financial prosperity.

In the realms of long-term investment and contrarian wisdom, you epitomize patience, discipline, and the courage to chart your course even when the tides of consensus seem insurmountable.

To those who humbly learn from both triumphs and setbacks, deriving wisdom from the tales of success and lessons from the echoes of failure, your willingness to grow and adapt is truly inspiring.

May the knowledge within these pages be a guiding light, illuminating your path through the complex landscape of the stock market. May your decisions be rooted in clarity, wisdom, and the understanding that every investment is a step toward building a brighter financial future.

With the deepest gratitude for your dedication to learning, growing, and shaping your financial destiny,

C. P. Kumar

CONTENTS

PREFACE

Welcome to the enthralling world of stock market investing! In this dynamic realm of finance, fortunes are made and lost, opportunities abound, and knowledge is the ultimate currency. Whether you're a seasoned investor seeking to refine your strategies or a novice eager to embark on your investment journey, "Investment Guide for the Stock Market" is your gateway to understanding the intricacies of this captivating landscape.

Imagine having the power to make informed decisions, confidently navigating the ebbs and flows of the market, and building a resilient portfolio that stands the test of time. This comprehensive guide is designed to empower you with the knowledge and tools necessary to achieve just that. Embark on a transformative voyage as we journey through the fundamental concepts that underpin successful stock market investing.

In the opening chapters, we'll lay the foundation with a bird's-eye view of the stock market's purpose and inner workings. From there, we'll dive into the crucial distinction between investment and speculation, unraveling the threads that tie long-term commitment to the art of making quick gains.

Our exploration takes us deeper into the world of market indices, those gauges that measure the heartbeat of the market. Understanding these indices is like reading the market's pulse, providing insights into its health and vitality. As we continue, we'll uncover the fascinating rhythm of market cycles and trends, teaching you how to discern patterns that can guide your choices.

Risk and reward, those inseparable companions, will take center stage as we examine their intricate dance in the context of stock investing. We'll show you how to achieve a delicate equilibrium, balancing the allure of gains with the prudence of risk management.

The heart of this guide beats within the realms of fundamental and technical analysis. We'll show you how to dissect a company's financial health and growth potential, while also delving into the world of charts, indicators, and price predictions. Discover the timeless wisdom of value investing and the promise of growth investing, each a unique path to uncovering hidden gems in the market.

Yet, investing is not just a science - it's an art, shaped by human psychology and the quirks of the mind. We'll embark on a fascinating journey into the psychology of investing, exploring how emotions can both elevate and undermine our decision-making. Through this lens, we'll confront behavioral biases head-on, equipping you with strategies to make rational choices.

But it's not just about mastering the market; it's about mastering yourself. Emotional intelligence becomes your secret weapon as we unveil how self-awareness and control can elevate your investing game. We'll explore diversification, asset allocation, and the art of portfolio rebalancing, guiding you in crafting a portfolio that weathers storms and thrives in the sun.

As we journey through these pages, you'll be introduced to the wisdom of long-term investing and the daring contrarian spirit that goes against the crowd. From triumphs to setbacks, real-life case studies will illuminate the path, ensuring that every experience - success or failure - becomes a stepping stone toward mastery.

The stock market is a symphony of numbers, emotions, and endless possibilities. "Investment Guide for the Stock Market" is your conductor's baton, guiding you through the crescendos and decrescendos of this grand financial performance. So, let the journey commence - a journey that promises not just financial growth, but also personal empowerment and enlightenment.

Get ready to transform your understanding of investing, one page at a time.

Happy reading and prosperous investing!

C. P. Kumar
Reiki Healer
Former Scientist 'G', National Institute of Hydrology
Roorkee - 247667, India
E-mail: cpkumar@yahoo.com
Web: https://www.angelfire.com/nh/cpkumar/virgo.html

Chapter 1. Introduction to Stock Market Investing

In today's complex financial landscape, where individuals seek avenues to grow their wealth and secure their financial future, the stock market has emerged as one of the most prominent and dynamic investment opportunities. This chapter serves as a comprehensive introduction to stock market investing, elucidating its fundamental concepts, purpose, and mechanics.

Understanding the Stock Market

The stock market, often referred to as the equity market, is a centralized platform where individuals and institutions buy and sell shares of publicly listed companies. These shares represent ownership in the company and entitle shareholders to a portion of its profits and assets. The stock market acts as a vital nexus connecting companies in need of capital to expand and investors looking to deploy their funds to generate returns.

Purpose of the Stock Market

The primary purpose of the stock market is to facilitate capital formation and allocation. It provides companies with a means to raise funds by issuing shares to the public. This infusion of capital allows companies to invest in research, development, expansion, and other strategic initiatives that drive economic growth.

For investors, the stock market offers a platform to allocate their savings and invest in companies they believe have the potential for growth and profitability. Investing in the stock market presents an opportunity to grow wealth over time, outpacing the rate of inflation and potentially achieving financial goals such as retirement, education, or wealth preservation.

Functioning of the Stock Market

The stock market operates within a structured framework, involving various participants and mechanisms that enable the buying and selling of securities. Here's an overview of how the stock market functions:

1. Companies Issue Initial Public Offerings (IPOs)

When a private company decides to go public, it conducts an Initial Public Offering (IPO). During an IPO, the company issues shares of stock to the public for the first time, allowing individuals and institutional investors to become shareholders.

2. Listing on Exchanges

Publicly traded companies list their shares on stock exchanges such as the New York Stock Exchange (NYSE) or the NASDAQ. These exchanges provide a regulated marketplace where buyers and sellers can transact shares. Each exchange has its listing requirements, which companies must meet to ensure transparency and credibility.

3. Role of Brokers

Individual investors cannot directly access the stock market; they require the services of brokerage firms. Brokers facilitate the buying and selling of securities on behalf of investors and charge a commission or fee for their services.

4. Placing Orders

Investors place orders through their chosen brokerage, specifying whether they want to buy or sell a particular stock, the quantity they wish to trade, and the price at which they are willing to transact. There are two main types of orders: market orders, which execute immediately at the current market price, and limit orders, which execute only at a specific price or better.

5. Bid and Ask Prices

Each stock has two key prices: the bid price and the ask price. The bid price is the highest price a buyer is willing to pay for a stock, while the ask price is the lowest price at which a seller is willing to part with their shares. The difference between the bid and ask prices is known as the bid-ask spread.

6. Matching Buyers and Sellers

Stock exchanges match buy and sell orders based on price and time priority. The exchange's trading system pairs compatible orders, ensuring a fair and efficient marketplace.

7. Market Indices

Market indices, such as the S&P 500 and the Dow Jones Industrial Average, are representative baskets of stocks used to gauge the overall performance of the stock market. These indices provide insights into market trends and investor sentiment.

Risks and Rewards of Stock Market Investing

While investing in the stock market offers the potential for substantial returns, it also carries inherent risks that investors must carefully consider.

1. Market Volatility

Stock prices can experience significant fluctuations over short periods due to various factors such as economic conditions, company performance, geopolitical events, and investor sentiment.

2. Risk of Loss

Investing in individual stocks involves the risk of loss if the company's performance deteriorates, leading to a decline in the stock's value. Some investments may even become worthless if the company goes bankrupt.

3. Diversification

Diversification, or spreading investments across various stocks and asset classes, is a strategy to mitigate risk. A well-diversified portfolio can help reduce the impact of poor performance by any single investment.

4. Research and Due Diligence

Successful stock market investing requires diligent research and analysis. Investors need to understand a company's financial health, competitive position, management team, and growth prospects before investing.

5. Long-Term Perspective

The stock market is best suited for investors with a long-term perspective. Short-term fluctuations are common, but historically, the market has shown an upward trajectory over extended periods.

Conclusion

The stock market serves as a dynamic arena where companies raise capital and investors seek opportunities for financial growth. Understanding the fundamentals of the stock market is crucial for individuals looking to venture into this realm of investment. As you embark on your journey in the stock market, remember that while it holds the potential for lucrative rewards, it demands careful consideration, research, and a long-term perspective to navigate the associated risks successfully. This chapter has provided you with a solid foundation to build upon as you delve deeper into the intricacies of stock market investing.

Chapter 2. Investment vs. Speculation

Introduction

In the fast-paced world of the stock market, two distinct approaches vie for attention: investment and speculation. While both involve capitalizing on market movements, they are fundamentally different in their objectives, time horizons, and risk tolerance. In this chapter of the book "Investment Guide for the Stock Market," we delve into the nuanced differences between long-term investing and short-term speculation. By understanding these differences, readers will be better equipped to make informed decisions and navigate the complexities of the stock market with wisdom.

Defining Investment and Speculation

1. Investment: Planting Seeds for Future Growth

At its core, investment is the strategic allocation of capital with the intention of generating returns over an extended period. The primary focus of investing is to achieve long-term financial goals, such as retirement planning, wealth preservation, or funding major life events. Investors seek out companies with strong fundamentals, solid growth prospects, and the potential to provide regular income through dividends.

2. Speculation: Riding the Volatile Waves

Speculation, on the other hand, involves making short-term bets on market fluctuations with the goal of profiting from price changes. Speculators are less concerned with a company's fundamentals and more interested in market sentiment, trends, and short-term price movements. The objective of speculation is to take advantage of rapid price swings and capitalize on market inefficiencies.

Time Horizon: Patience vs. Impulsivity

1. Investment: Cultivating Patience for Long-Term Growth

Long-term investing requires a patient outlook. Investors understand that the stock market experiences natural ebbs and flows over time, and they are willing to weather short-term volatility for the potential of substantial gains in the future. The emphasis is on buying and holding quality assets for years, if not decades.

2. Speculation: Seizing Opportunities in the Moment

Speculators, in contrast, thrive on short-term opportunities. They are driven by the desire to capitalize on quick market movements, often buying and selling stocks within a matter of days or even hours. Speculation demands a keen sense of timing and the ability to make swift decisions in response to rapidly changing market conditions.

Risk Tolerance: Stability vs. Roller-Coaster

1. Investment: Embracing Stability and Diversification

Investors tend to have a more risk-averse approach. They prioritize stability and aim to minimize the impact of market downturns. Diversification, spreading investments across different asset classes and industries, is a key strategy for mitigating risk. By holding a diverse portfolio of investments, investors can cushion the impact of poor performance in any single asset.

2. Speculation: Riding the Roller-Coaster of Risk

Speculators knowingly embrace higher levels of risk. Their strategies are often concentrated, focusing on a few select stocks or even specific market sectors. While this approach can yield substantial gains in the short term, it also exposes speculators to the potential for significant losses. Speculators must be prepared to handle the emotional and financial challenges that come with heightened risk exposure.

Research and Analysis: Fundamentals vs. Market Trends

1. Investment: Delving into Fundamentals

Investors delve deep into a company's financial health, examining its balance sheets, income statements, and cash flow reports. Fundamental analysis is a cornerstone of investment decision-making, as it provides insights into a company's value and growth potential over time. Investors seek to align their investments with companies that demonstrate strong earnings growth, competitive advantages, and sustainable business models.

2. Speculation: Riding the Waves of Market Sentiment

Speculators focus more on technical analysis and market trends. They analyze historical price movements, trading volumes, and patterns to predict short-term price fluctuations. Market sentiment and news play a crucial role in speculators' decisions, as they aim to capitalize on the psychology of other market participants. Unlike investors, speculators are less concerned with a company's intrinsic value and more interested in profiting from short-term market movements.

Emotional Resilience: Steadfastness vs. Quick Reactions

1. Investment: Cultivating Steadfastness

Investing requires emotional resilience. Long-term investors need to remain steadfast in their convictions even when faced with market downturns. By focusing on the underlying value of their investments and their long-term goals, investors can avoid making impulsive decisions based on short-term market fluctuations.

2. Speculation: Navigating Quick Reactions

Speculators must navigate their emotions with agility. The fast-paced nature of speculation can lead to impulsive decisions driven by fear or greed. Successful speculators develop a disciplined approach, setting clear entry and exit points for their trades and adhering to a well-defined strategy even in the face of rapid market changes.

Conclusion

In the world of the stock market, the distinction between investment and speculation is not just a matter of terminology - it's a fundamental difference in approach, mindset, and objectives. Long-term investing and short-term speculation cater to different risk appetites, time horizons, and levels of emotional resilience. As readers embark on their journey through the stock market, armed with the knowledge and insights presented in this chapter, they can make informed choices that align with their financial goals, risk tolerance, and investment philosophy. Whether choosing the patient path of investment or the fast-paced realm of speculation, understanding these approaches empowers individuals to navigate the market landscape with wisdom and prudence.

Chapter 3. Understanding Market Indices

Introduction

In the dynamic world of the stock market, understanding the performance and trends can often be a complex task. This is where market indices come to the rescue. Market indices provide investors with a snapshot of how a particular segment of the stock market is performing. They act as benchmarks, helping investors gauge the overall direction of the market and make informed decisions. In this chapter, we delve into the world of market indices, exploring their types, significance, and how investors can leverage this essential tool to navigate the stock market landscape.

What are Market Indices?

Market indices, simply put, are statistical measures designed to reflect the performance of a specific group of stocks within the stock market. These indices serve as indicators, representing the overall health and direction of the market segment they track. By analyzing the movements of market indices, investors can gain valuable insights into the broader market trends.

Composition of Market Indices

Market indices consist of a selected basket of stocks that meet certain criteria. These criteria might include factors like market capitalization, industry sector, liquidity, and trading volume. The goal is to create a representative sample of stocks that mirror the performance of the broader market or a specific sector.

For example, a market index tracking the technology sector would comprise tech-related companies like Apple, Microsoft, and Google. Similarly, an index representing the healthcare sector might include companies such as Pfizer, Johnson & Johnson, and Merck.

Significance of Market Indices

Market indices play a pivotal role in the world of investing, providing both seasoned investors and newcomers with valuable information. Here are some key reasons why market indices hold such significance:

1. Tracking Overall Market Performance

One of the primary purposes of market indices is to provide a snapshot of the overall market performance. The movement of these indices gives investors a sense of whether the market is experiencing growth, decline, or stability. A rising index generally indicates a bullish market, while a declining index suggests a bearish market sentiment.

2. Benchmarking and Comparison

Market indices also serve as benchmarks against which individual portfolios can be measured. Investors can compare the performance of their investments with that of relevant indices to assess their portfolio's relative strength. This benchmarking process helps investors gauge the effectiveness of their investment strategies and make necessary adjustments.

3. Sector and Industry Insights

Market indices are not limited to reflecting the overall market. They can also provide insights into specific sectors or industries. For instance, a sector-specific index can reveal whether a particular industry is outperforming or underperforming the broader market. This information can be valuable for investors looking to allocate their funds strategically.

4. Market Sentiment Indicators

The movement of market indices can also reflect the prevailing market sentiment. Rapid changes in an index might suggest increased market volatility or a reaction to significant economic or geopolitical events. By monitoring these movements, investors can anticipate potential market shifts and adjust their strategies accordingly.

Types of Market Indices

Market indices come in various types, each designed to cater to different investment preferences and objectives. Understanding the different types of indices can aid investors in selecting the ones that align with their goals. Here are some common types of market indices:

1. Broad Market Indices

Broad market indices, often referred to as "total market" indices, aim to capture the performance of the entire stock market. These indices encompass a wide range of companies across various sectors and industries. Examples of broad market indices include the S&P 500, which tracks 500 large-cap U.S. companies, and the Wilshire 5000, which covers nearly all publicly traded U.S. stocks.

2. Sectoral Indices

Sectoral indices focus on specific industry sectors, allowing investors to gauge the performance of a particular segment of the market. Examples include the Nasdaq Biotechnology Index, which tracks biotech companies, and the Dow Jones U.S. Real Estate Index, which monitors real estate companies.

3. International Indices

International indices provide insights into the performance of stock markets in different countries or regions. These indices are valuable for investors looking to diversify their portfolios globally. The FTSE All-World ex-US Index, for instance, covers stocks from various countries excluding the United States.

4. Style Indices

Style indices categorize stocks based on their investment styles, such as value, growth, or a blend of both. The Russell 1000 Growth Index and the Russell 1000 Value Index are examples of style indices that track growth-oriented and value-oriented companies, respectively.

5. Size Indices

Size indices classify stocks by their market capitalization, grouping them as small-cap, mid-cap, or large-cap. These indices can help investors focus on specific segments of the market based on the size of the companies. The Russell 2000 Index, for instance, tracks small-cap U.S. companies.

Interpreting Market Index Movements

Interpreting the movements of market indices requires a nuanced understanding of various factors that influence the stock market. While a rising index generally suggests positive market sentiment, and a declining index might signal a downturn, there are additional considerations to keep in mind:

1. Market Factors vs. Index-Specific Factors

It's important to distinguish between factors that affect the entire market and those specific to a particular index. For example, an economic downturn might impact most indices, but a sector-specific development could significantly influence a sectoral index.

2. Index Composition Changes

Market indices periodically update their composition to reflect changes in the underlying stocks. New companies may be added, while others might be removed. These changes can affect the performance of the index and need to be considered when analyzing its movements.

3. External Influences

Market indices can be influenced by various external factors, including macroeconomic indicators, geopolitical events, interest rate changes, and global market trends. Understanding how these factors impact the broader market can provide context for interpreting index movements.

Leveraging Market Indices for Investment Strategies

Market indices are powerful tools that investors can use to shape their investment strategies. Here's how investors can leverage these indices for their benefit.

1. Portfolio Diversification

By investing in index funds or exchange-traded funds (ETFs) that track market indices, investors can achieve instant diversification. These funds mirror the performance of the index they're based on, providing exposure to a wide range of stocks within a specific category.

2. Tactical Asset Allocation

Investors can use market indices to adjust their asset allocation strategy based on market trends. For instance, if a sectoral index is performing well, an investor might choose to allocate more funds to that sector.

3. Long-Term Investment

For long-term investors, broad market indices can serve as a foundation for portfolio growth. Historical data indicates that the overall trend of the stock market is upward over extended periods, making long-term investments in broad market indices potentially rewarding.

4. Market Insights

By regularly monitoring market indices, investors can gain insights into the market's sentiment and direction. This information can guide them in making timely decisions to optimize their investment positions.

Conclusion

In the intricate world of stock market dynamics, market indices emerge as invaluable tools that empower investors with insights, benchmarks, and strategies to navigate the complex landscape. These indices, composed of carefully selected stocks meeting specific criteria, encapsulate the essence of market segments and provide a panoramic view of trends.

Market indices hold multifaceted significance, serving as compasses guiding investors through uncertain terrain. Their ability to track overall market performance, offer benchmarking for portfolios, provide sector-specific insights, and reflect market sentiment is pivotal. By deciphering the movements of indices, investors can make informed decisions, adapting to changing market conditions.

The diverse array of market indices encompasses broad market indices, sectoral indices, international indices, style indices, and size indices, catering to diverse investment goals. Understanding the nuanced interplay of factors influencing index movements is vital. Differentiating between market-wide influences, index-specific changes, and external catalysts ensures a comprehensive interpretation of trends.

Leveraging market indices is a potent strategy in an investor's arsenal. Employing index funds or ETFs for diversification, adapting asset allocation based on index performance, embracing long-term investment through broad market indices, and mining insights for timely decisions are all ways to harness the power of indices.

In a world characterized by market flux, market indices stand as pillars of stability, offering a steady pulse amidst volatility. Armed with a deeper understanding of these indices, investors are better equipped to traverse the complex landscape of the stock market, turning uncertainty into opportunity and data into informed action.

Chapter 4. Market Cycles and Trends

Introduction

In the fast-paced world of stock trading, it's crucial for investors to understand the cyclical nature of the market and the trends that shape it. Market cycles and trends play a significant role in determining the direction of stock prices, and having a solid grasp of these dynamics can greatly enhance one's ability to make informed investment decisions. In this chapter, we will delve into the intricacies of market cycles, explore how to identify trends, and discuss strategies for capitalizing on these patterns.

The Nature of Market Cycles

1. The Four Phases

Market cycles are the recurring patterns of price movement that occur in financial markets. These cycles typically consist of four phases:

Accumulation Phase: This marks the beginning of a new cycle. During this phase, smart money investors and institutions start accumulating stocks that have been beaten down in the previous cycle. Prices are relatively low, and investor sentiment is pessimistic.

Uptrend Phase: As buying activity increases, the market enters an uptrend phase. This is characterized by steady price appreciation, often driven by improving economic fundamentals and positive sentiment. Retail investors start to notice the upward movement and may begin to participate.

Distribution Phase: At the peak of an uptrend, the market enters a distribution phase. During this period, smart money investors start selling their positions to capitalize on the price gains. Retail investors often join the frenzy, driving prices even higher. However, underlying fundamentals may not support these inflated prices.

Downtrend Phase: The distribution phase gives way to a downtrend phase, where prices start declining. Panic selling and negative sentiment dominate as investors rush to exit positions. This phase clears out the excesses of the previous uptrend and sets the stage for a new accumulation phase.

2. Duration and Variability

It's important to note that market cycles are not set in stone, and their durations can vary significantly. Some cycles might last a few months, while others can span several years. External factors such as economic events, geopolitical tensions, and technological advancements can influence the length and intensity of each cycle.

Identifying Market Trends

1. Technical Analysis

Technical analysis is a widely used approach to identify and predict market trends. It involves analyzing price charts, volume, and other market indicators to make informed predictions about future price movements. Some key concepts in technical analysis include:

Trendlines: Trendlines are drawn on price charts to identify the general direction of the market. An upward trendline connects higher lows, while a downward trendline connects lower highs.

Moving Averages: Moving averages smooth out price data and help identify the underlying trend. The 50-day and 200-day moving averages are commonly used by traders to determine the overall trend direction.

Support and Resistance Levels: These levels indicate where prices are likely to encounter buying (support) or selling (resistance) pressure. Traders use these levels to make decisions about entry and exit points.

2. Fundamental Analysis

Fundamental analysis focuses on evaluating a company's financial health and economic indicators to predict future stock prices. By analyzing factors such as earnings, revenue growth, debt levels, and industry trends, investors can gain insights into the potential direction of a stock's price.

Earnings Reports: Quarterly earnings reports provide a snapshot of a company's financial performance. Positive earnings surprises can lead to price increases, while disappointments can result in declines.

Economic Indicators: Macroeconomic indicators, such as GDP growth, unemployment rates, and inflation, can impact the overall market trend. Positive economic data may lead to an uptrend, while negative data can contribute to a downtrend.

Industry Trends: Understanding the broader trends and dynamics within an industry can help investors identify potential winners and losers. Industries that are growing rapidly tend to have companies with better earnings prospects, leading to upward trends.

Strategies for Capitalizing on Trends

1. Trend Following

Trend following is a strategy where investors capitalize on existing market trends by buying when the market is in an uptrend and selling when it's in a downtrend. This approach relies on the belief that trends tend to persist over time.

Moving Average Crossovers: When a shorter-term moving average crosses above a longer-term moving average, it signals a potential uptrend and a buying opportunity. Conversely, a cross below may indicate a downtrend and a selling opportunity.

Trend Confirmation Indicators: Technical indicators like the Relative Strength Index (RSI) and Moving Average Convergence Divergence (MACD) can provide additional confirmation of a trend's strength before making a trade. RSI is a momentum oscillator that measures the speed and change of price movements to indicate overbought or oversold conditions in a market. MACD is a trend-following momentum indicator that shows the relationship between two moving averages of a security's price, helping to identify potential buy or sell signals.

2. Contrarian Strategies

Contrarian strategies involve going against the prevailing market sentiment. Contrarian investors believe that the market often overreacts to news and events, leading to mispricings that can be exploited.

Buy the Dip: This strategy involves buying stocks when they experience sharp declines due to negative news or market corrections. Contrarians assume that these downturns are temporary and offer buying opportunities.

Value Investing: Value investors seek out stocks that are undervalued based on fundamental analysis. They believe that the market will eventually recognize the true value of the company, leading to price appreciation.

Managing Risks in Trend Trading

1. Diversification

Diversification is a risk management strategy that involves spreading investments across different assets and sectors. This approach helps mitigate the impact of a single stock's poor performance on the overall portfolio.

2. Stop-Loss Orders

Stop-loss orders are instructions to sell a stock if its price reaches a certain level. These orders help limit potential losses by automatically executing a trade when the stock price moves against the desired trend.

3. Risk-Reward Ratio

Before making a trade, investors should assess the potential risk and reward of the trade. The risk-reward ratio helps investors determine whether a trade is worth pursuing based on the potential profit compared to the potential loss.

Conclusion

Understanding market cycles and trends is essential for successful investing in the stock market. By recognizing the cyclical nature of markets, identifying trends through technical and fundamental analysis, and employing effective trading strategies, investors can make informed decisions that have the potential to yield positive returns. It's important to remember that while trends can provide valuable insights, no strategy can eliminate all risks. Therefore, a well-rounded approach that combines research, analysis, and risk management is key to navigating the complex world of stock market investing.

Chapter 5. Risk and Return Relationship

Introduction

Investing in the stock market can be both exhilarating and nerve-wracking. The prospect of earning substantial returns is alluring, but the fear of losing hard-earned money can be equally daunting. This chapter delves into a fundamental aspect of investing: the intricate relationship between risk and potential returns. Understanding this relationship is essential for investors seeking to navigate the stock market with confidence and make informed decisions. We will explore how risk and return are intertwined, strategies to balance them effectively, and the tools investors can employ to assess and manage risk.

The Foundation of Investing: Risk and Return

At the core of every investment decision lies the trade-off between risk and potential returns. Risk represents the uncertainty or variability of returns associated with an investment, while return refers to the gains an investor hopes to achieve. The two are inextricably linked: higher potential returns often come with higher levels of risk, and lower risk usually corresponds to more modest potential returns.

Understanding Risk Types in Stock Investing

Not all risks in stock investing are the same. It's crucial to distinguish between various types of risks that investors encounter:

Market Risk (Systematic Risk): This risk stems from factors affecting the entire market, such as economic downturns, geopolitical events, or interest rate changes. Market risk cannot be eliminated through diversification and impacts all investments to some degree.

Company-Specific Risk (Unsystematic Risk): These risks are unique to a specific company or industry. Examples include management changes, technological disruptions, or regulatory issues. Diversification across different companies and sectors can help mitigate company-specific risk.

Liquidity Risk: Liquidity risk arises when an investor cannot quickly sell an investment without a significant price reduction. Stocks with low trading volumes may pose liquidity challenges.

Currency Risk: For international investments, fluctuations in currency exchange rates can impact returns. Investors need to consider this risk when investing in foreign stocks.

Interest Rate Risk: Changes in interest rates can influence stock prices. When interest rates rise, investors may shift their preferences to fixed-income investments, affecting stock prices.

Risk Tolerance and Investment Goals

An investor's risk tolerance is a critical factor in determining the right balance between risk and return. Risk tolerance is influenced by factors such as financial situation, time horizon, investment goals, and psychological disposition. Different individuals have varying levels of comfort with risk, and it's crucial to align investment decisions with one's risk tolerance and long-term objectives.

The Risk-Return Trade-Off

The risk-return trade-off is a foundational principle in finance that highlights the direct relationship between risk and potential returns. In general, investments with higher potential returns tend to carry greater levels of risk, while safer investments with lower risk offer relatively modest potential returns. Striking the right balance depends on an investor's risk tolerance and financial goals.

Balancing Risk and Return: Strategies for Investors

Diversification: Diversifying a portfolio across different asset classes, sectors, and geographical regions can help mitigate risks associated with individual investments. A well-diversified portfolio is less vulnerable to the impact of a single company's poor performance or adverse events in a specific industry.

Asset Allocation: Asset allocation involves determining the proportion of your portfolio invested in various asset classes, such as stocks, bonds, and cash equivalents. Adjusting asset allocation based on risk tolerance and market conditions is a strategic way to manage risk and return.

Risk Management Tools: Investors can use various tools to manage risk, including stop-loss orders, which automatically trigger a sale if a stock's price falls to a certain level. Options and derivatives can also be employed to hedge against potential losses.

Long-Term Perspective: The stock market tends to be volatile in the short term, but historical data indicates that it generally trends upward over the long term. Maintaining a long-term perspective can help investors ride out short-term fluctuations and reduce the impact of market volatility on their portfolios.

Measuring and Assessing Risk

Evaluating the risk associated with an investment is a crucial step in making informed decisions. Some common tools for measuring risk include:

Standard Deviation: This statistical measure quantifies the degree of variability in an investment's returns. A higher standard deviation indicates greater risk.

Beta: Beta measures a stock's sensitivity to market movements. A beta of 1 suggests the stock moves in line with the market, while a beta greater than 1 indicates higher volatility.

Value at Risk (VaR): VaR estimates the potential loss an investment may experience within a specific confidence level and time frame. It helps investors gauge the worst-case scenario.

Conclusion

The risk and return relationship lies at the heart of investment decisions in the stock market. As investors seek to maximize returns while managing risk, understanding the types of risks, evaluating risk tolerance, and employing strategies such as diversification and asset allocation are paramount. By approaching the stock market with a comprehensive understanding of this dynamic relationship, investors can navigate the ups and downs with greater confidence and increase their potential for long-term success. Remember, while risk cannot be completely eliminated, prudent risk management can lead to a more rewarding investment journey.

Chapter 6. Fundamental Analysis

Introduction

In the dynamic world of stock market investing, it's essential to have a solid understanding of the companies you're considering for investment. Fundamental analysis provides a comprehensive framework for evaluating a company's financial health, earnings potential, and growth prospects. This chapter will delve into the intricacies of fundamental analysis, helping you make informed decisions and navigate the stock market with confidence.

Understanding Fundamental Analysis

Fundamental analysis is a cornerstone of intelligent investing. Unlike technical analysis, which focuses on stock price patterns and market trends, fundamental analysis centers on a company's underlying financial and economic factors. By scrutinizing a company's financial statements and other relevant data, investors can gain insights into the company's true value and potential for growth.

The Core Components of Fundamental Analysis

Fundamental analysis involves an in-depth examination of several key components that collectively shape a company's financial health and growth prospects.

1. Financial Statements: The Building Blocks

At the heart of fundamental analysis are a company's financial statements – the balance sheet, income statement, and cash flow statement. These documents provide a comprehensive snapshot of a company's financial position, performance, and cash flows.

Balance Sheet: This statement presents a company's assets, liabilities, and shareholders' equity, providing a clear view of its financial position at a specific point in time. By analyzing the balance sheet, investors can assess a company's solvency and liquidity.

Income Statement: Also known as the profit and loss statement, the income statement displays a company's revenues, expenses, and profits over a specified period. This statement offers insights into a company's profitability and operating efficiency.

Cash Flow Statement: The cash flow statement outlines the movement of cash into and out of a company during a given period. It reveals the company's ability to generate cash and meet its financial obligations.

2. Earnings and Profitability

Earnings play a pivotal role in evaluating a company's financial performance and growth potential. Key metrics such as earnings per share (EPS), price-to-earnings (P/E) ratio, and return on equity (ROE) shed light on how efficiently a company generates profits and rewards its shareholders.

Earnings Per Share (EPS): EPS indicates the portion of a company's profits allocated to each outstanding share of its stock. Higher EPS values generally reflect better profitability.

Price-to-Earnings (P/E) Ratio: The P/E ratio compares a company's stock price to its earnings per share. It serves as a valuation metric, highlighting the market's expectations for future growth.

Return on Equity (ROE): ROE measures a company's ability to generate returns for its shareholders based on the equity invested. A higher ROE often indicates effective management and efficient capital utilization.

3. Growth Prospects and Dividends

Investors are keenly interested in a company's potential for future growth. Analyzing a company's historical growth rates, as well as its plans for expansion and innovation, can provide valuable insights into its long-term prospects.

Historical Growth Rates: Reviewing a company's historical revenue and earnings growth rates can reveal patterns and trends that might continue in the future.

Dividend History: Some investors seek stable income through dividends. A company's dividend history and its ability to sustain and grow dividends are essential considerations for income-focused investors.

The Process of Fundamental Analysis

Fundamental analysis is a systematic process that involves several steps to evaluate a company's financial health and growth potential.

1. Gathering Data and Information

Start by collecting the necessary data, including financial statements, annual reports, and news releases. Online financial databases and company websites are valuable sources of information.

2. Financial Statement Analysis

Carefully analyze the balance sheet, income statement, and cash flow statement. Look for trends, anomalies, and key ratios that offer insights into the company's financial health.

3. Evaluating Ratios and Metrics

Calculate and evaluate key financial ratios and metrics, such as debt-to-equity ratio, current ratio, and P/E ratio. Compare these metrics with industry averages to gain a broader perspective.

4. Assessing Growth Potential

Study the company's growth prospects, including its industry position, competitive advantage, and potential for innovation. Analyze historical growth rates and consider the impact of industry trends.

5. Industry and Market Analysis

Understand the broader industry dynamics and market trends that could affect the company's performance. External factors, such as changes in consumer behavior or technological advancements, can significantly impact a company's fortunes.

6. Management and Corporate Governance

Examine the company's management team and their track record. Effective leadership and corporate governance play a crucial role in a company's success.

Challenges and Limitations of Fundamental Analysis

While fundamental analysis offers valuable insights, it's important to acknowledge its limitations.

1. Data Accuracy and Reliability

Fundamental analysis heavily relies on accurate and reliable financial data. However, discrepancies or misreporting can lead to incorrect assessments.

2. Subjectivity and Interpretation

Interpreting financial statements and ratios involves a degree of subjectivity. Different analysts may arrive at varying conclusions based on their interpretations.

3. Macro-Economic Factors

External macro-economic factors, such as changes in interest rates, inflation, and geopolitical events, can impact a company's performance despite its sound fundamentals.

Conclusion

Fundamental analysis provides a comprehensive framework for evaluating a company's financial health and growth prospects. By delving into financial statements, assessing key ratios, and studying growth potential, investors can make informed decisions that align with their investment goals. However, it's crucial to recognize that fundamental analysis is just one piece of the investment puzzle. Combining it with other approaches and staying attuned to market trends will help you navigate the stock market effectively and achieve your investment objectives.

Chapter 7. Technical Analysis

Introduction

In the dynamic world of stock trading, where prices can be influenced by a multitude of factors ranging from global economic trends to company-specific news, investors seek tools and strategies that can help them navigate the uncertain terrain and make informed decisions. One of the key methodologies employed by traders and investors is Technical Analysis. In this chapter, we delve into the realm of technical analysis, exploring its principles, tools, and applications in predicting price movements in the stock market.

Understanding Technical Analysis

Technical analysis is a methodology used to analyze historical price and volume data of stocks to predict future price movements. Unlike fundamental analysis, which focuses on a company's financials and underlying value, technical analysis is centered on chart patterns, indicators, and other tools that provide insights into market sentiment and potential trends.

The Premise of Technical Analysis

At the core of technical analysis lies the belief that historical price patterns tend to repeat themselves due to the collective behavior of market participants. This means that by studying past price movements, investors can gain insights into the psychology of the market and make more informed decisions.

Chart Patterns: Decoding Price Movement

Chart patterns are visual representations of price movements over time. These patterns can offer valuable insights into potential future price movements. Some of the most common chart patterns include:

1. Head and Shoulders

This pattern signals a potential reversal in the trend. It consists of three peaks, with the central peak being the highest (the head), flanked by two lower peaks (the shoulders). A break below the neckline often indicates a downward trend.

2. Double Top and Double Bottom

These patterns represent a reversal in trend as well. A double top consists of two peaks of similar height, while a double bottom comprises two troughs. These patterns suggest a shift in sentiment from bullish to bearish or vice versa.

3. Triangles

Symmetrical, ascending, and descending triangles indicate potential trend continuation. Breakouts from these patterns can provide valuable trading signals.

4. Cup and Handle

This pattern resembles a tea cup, with a rounded bottom followed by a small consolidation (the handle). It suggests a bullish continuation after the handle's breakout.

Technical Indicators: Insights from Data Analysis

Technical indicators are mathematical calculations derived from price and volume data. They offer insights into market trends and potential turning points. Some popular technical indicators include:

1. Moving Averages

Moving averages smooth out price data to identify trends. The simple moving average (SMA) calculates the average price over a specified period, while the exponential moving average (EMA) gives more weight to recent prices.

2. Relative Strength Index (RSI)

The RSI measures the speed and change of price movements. It ranges from 0 to 100 and indicates whether a stock is overbought (above 70) or oversold (below 30).

3. Moving Average Convergence Divergence (MACD)

The MACD is a trend-following momentum indicator that shows the relationship between two moving averages of a stock's price. It consists of the MACD line, signal line, and histogram.

The MACD line is the difference between the 12-period Exponential Moving Average (EMA) and the 26-period EMA. It serves as a measure of the short-term and longer-term trends in a security's price movement. The signal line is an EMA applied to the MACD line itself. It helps smooth out the MACD line and generates trading signals when it crosses above or below the MACD line. The histogram is a graphical representation of the difference between the MACD line and the signal Line. It oscillates above and below a zero line, indicating the strength and direction of the momentum. A positive histogram suggests bullish momentum, while a negative histogram indicates bearish momentum.

4. Bollinger Bands

Bollinger Bands consist of a moving average, an upper band (usually two standard deviations above the moving average), and a lower band (two standard deviations below the moving average). They provide insights into volatility and potential price reversals.

Oscillators and Momentum Indicators: Gauging Price Speed

Oscillators and momentum indicators are a subset of technical indicators that help identify overbought and oversold conditions and assess the speed of price movements.

1. Stochastic Oscillator

The stochastic oscillator compares a stock's closing price to its price range over a specific period. It ranges from 0 to 100 and indicates potential reversal points.

2. Commodity Channel Index (CCI)

The CCI measures a stock's deviation from its statistical average. It helps identify overbought and oversold conditions.

3. Average Directional Index (ADX)

The ADX determines the strength of a trend rather than its direction. It ranges from 0 to 100 and helps traders assess the viability of a trend.

Applying Technical Analysis: Strategies and Considerations

While technical analysis provides valuable insights, it's important to recognize its limitations and use it in conjunction with other analysis methods. Here are some strategies and considerations when applying technical analysis:

1. Multiple Indicators

Using a combination of indicators can provide a more comprehensive view of a stock's potential movement. However, avoid overwhelming yourself with too many indicators, as they might provide conflicting signals.

2. Timeframes

Different timeframes reveal different aspects of price movements. Short-term traders might focus on intraday charts, while long-term investors might analyze weekly or monthly charts.

3. Confirmation from Volume

Volume can validate the strength of a price movement. Increasing volume during a breakout can signify strong market participation.

4. News and Events

Technical analysis might not account for sudden price movements due to unexpected news or events. Stay updated on company-specific and market-wide news.

The Psychological Aspect: Market Sentiment and Behavior

Technical analysis isn't solely about crunching numbers; it's also about understanding the psychology of market participants. Recognizing patterns formed by market sentiment can provide insights into potential price movements.

1. Support and Resistance Levels

Support levels indicate where a stock's price has historically stopped falling, while resistance levels mark where it has paused its upward movement. These levels are influenced by market psychology.

2. Fear and Greed

Market sentiment is often driven by fear and greed. Recognizing these emotional factors can help traders make more informed decisions.

Conclusion

Technical analysis offers traders and investors a valuable toolkit to navigate the complexities of the stock market. By studying chart patterns, utilizing indicators, and understanding market sentiment, practitioners of technical analysis aim to predict future price movements. However, it's important to remember that no analysis method is foolproof. Combining technical analysis with other strategies, staying informed about news and events, and considering the psychological aspects of trading can help improve decision-making in the ever-evolving world of stock trading.

Chapter 8. Value Investing

Introduction

In the dynamic world of stock market investing, where trends can shift swiftly and unpredictably, value investing stands as a steadfast strategy rooted in timeless principles. The approach, popularized by legendary investor Warren Buffett, centers on identifying and investing in undervalued stocks with the potential to provide substantial returns over the long term. This chapter delves into the principles of value investing and offers insights into how investors can effectively identify undervalued stocks for their portfolios.

Understanding Value Investing

Value investing is a philosophy that seeks to capitalize on market inefficiencies, where certain stocks are temporarily mispriced due to market sentiment, short-term trends, or other external factors. The core principle of value investing revolves around the idea of purchasing these undervalued stocks, allowing investors to gain a competitive advantage by acquiring assets at a discount.

1. The Warren Buffett Influence

Warren Buffett, often referred to as the "Oracle of Omaha," is perhaps the most renowned practitioner of value investing. His success and wealth accumulation are testaments to the effectiveness of this strategy. Buffett's approach is grounded in the belief that the stock market occasionally misprices quality companies, presenting opportunities for astute investors to acquire shares at a lower cost than their intrinsic value.

2. Intrinsic Value and Margin of Safety

Central to value investing is the concept of "intrinsic value." Intrinsic value refers to the true worth of a company's shares, determined by its fundamentals, earnings potential, and growth prospects. Value investors seek to identify companies whose stock prices trade below their calculated intrinsic value.

A related principle is the "margin of safety." This involves investing in stocks with a significant gap between their market price and estimated intrinsic value. This cushion provides protection against potential losses and market fluctuations.

Identifying Undervalued Stocks

Identifying undervalued stocks is both an art and a science, requiring a comprehensive analysis of financial data, industry trends, and broader economic factors. Successful value investors employ a range of techniques to uncover hidden gems within the stock market.

1. Fundamental Analysis

Fundamental analysis is the cornerstone of value investing. It involves a thorough examination of a company's financial statements, including its balance sheet, income statement, and cash flow statement. Key metrics such as earnings per share (EPS), price-to-earnings (P/E) ratio, and price-to-book (P/B) ratio are used to assess a company's financial health and valuation.

Investors also analyze a company's competitive advantage, management team, and industry positioning. By evaluating these factors, investors can gauge whether a company's stock is trading at a discount compared to its intrinsic value.

2. Contrarian Thinking

Value investing often involves contrarian thinking, where investors go against prevailing market sentiment. When the market experiences downturns or pessimism surrounding a particular sector, value investors see an opportunity to purchase stocks that others are selling due to short-term fears. This approach requires patience and a long-term perspective, as stocks purchased during downturns may take time to rebound.

3. Picking Quality Companies

Value investing is not solely about finding cheap stocks; it's about finding undervalued stocks of high-quality companies. These are companies with strong competitive advantages, consistent earnings, and a history of sound management decisions. Investing in companies with these attributes can lead to long-term growth and stability.

Strategies for Value Investing

The art of value investing encompasses various strategies and techniques that investors can employ to build a portfolio of undervalued stocks with growth potential.

1. Dividend Investing

Dividend investing is a value-oriented strategy that involves seeking out companies that pay consistent and substantial dividends. These dividend payments provide a steady stream of income to investors, even during market downturns. Value investors often look for companies with a history of increasing dividends over time, as this is indicative of financial strength and management confidence.

2. Growth at a Reasonable Price (GARP)

The Growth at a Reasonable Price (GARP) strategy combines elements of both value and growth investing. Investors following this approach seek companies that exhibit strong growth potential but are trading at a reasonable valuation. GARP investors aim to find stocks that offer the best of both worlds – the potential for capital appreciation and a margin of safety.

3. Long-Term Horizon

Patience is a virtue in value investing. Successful practitioners of this strategy often have a long-term investment horizon, allowing time for the market to recognize the true value of their chosen stocks. By avoiding short-term fluctuations and focusing on the long-term prospects of a company, investors can benefit from the power of compounding and weather market volatility.

Risks and Challenges of Value Investing

While value investing can be highly rewarding, it's not without its risks and challenges.

1. Value Traps

Value traps occur when a stock appears to be undervalued but is actually facing fundamental issues that prevent it from realizing its potential. Investors must carefully assess whether a company's stock price decline is due to temporary setbacks or deep-rooted problems.

2. Market Timing

Timing the market is challenging, even for value investors. Stocks can remain undervalued for extended periods, and attempting to predict the optimal entry point can lead to missed opportunities or premature investments.

3. Psychological Biases

Value investing requires a strong psychological disposition. During market downturns, the fear and panic that affect the broader market can also impact value investors. Staying true to the principles of value investing and maintaining a long-term perspective can be difficult when surrounded by market turbulence.

Conclusion

Value investing remains a timeless investment philosophy that has stood the test of time. By seeking out undervalued stocks with solid fundamentals and long-term growth potential, investors can position themselves to achieve substantial returns. The principles pioneered by Warren Buffett continue to serve as guiding lights for investors navigating the complexities of the stock market. However, value investing is not a one-size-fits-all strategy, and careful research, analysis, and a patient approach are necessary for success. As investors embark on their journey to uncover hidden gems in the stock market, they should remember that value investing is a journey of learning and adaptation, where dedication and discipline pave the way to financial prosperity.

Chapter 9. Growth Investing

Introduction

In the dynamic world of stock market investing, there exists a strategy that seeks to capitalize on companies with high growth potential. This strategy, known as growth investing, involves identifying and investing in stocks of companies that are expected to experience rapid expansion and substantial earnings growth. While growth investing offers the allure of potentially significant returns, it also comes with its fair share of risks and challenges. In this chapter, we will delve into the key principles, strategies, benefits, and risks associated with growth investing.

Understanding Growth Investing

Growth investing is built on the premise of identifying companies that are poised for rapid expansion and increased profitability in the future. Unlike value investing, which focuses on stocks that appear undervalued relative to their intrinsic worth, growth investing seeks out companies with robust earnings growth and the potential to continue this trajectory over an extended period.

Key Characteristics of Growth Stocks

Growth stocks typically exhibit certain key characteristics that distinguish them from other investment categories:

1. Earnings Growth: Growth stocks are characterized by their ability to consistently deliver above-average earnings growth. These companies often reinvest their earnings into expanding operations, research and development, and innovation.

2. Innovative Products/Services: Many growth companies are at the forefront of innovation, introducing new and disruptive products or services to the market. Their ability to capture market share and generate demand can contribute to their growth potential.

3. Expanding Market Presence: Growth stocks often have a substantial share of a rapidly expanding market. Their ability to capture a larger portion of market demand contributes to their revenue growth.

4. High Valuations: Due to their perceived potential, growth stocks tend to trade at higher price-to-earnings (P/E) ratios compared to value stocks. Investors are willing to pay a premium for the growth prospects these companies offer.

Strategies for Growth Investing

Growth investing involves employing various strategies to identify and capitalize on companies with high growth potential. While no strategy guarantees success, a combination of the following approaches can help investors make informed decisions:

1. Fundamental Analysis

Fundamental analysis is a cornerstone of growth investing. This approach involves evaluating a company's financial health, management quality, competitive position, and growth prospects. Key metrics to consider include earnings per share (EPS) growth, revenue growth rate, return on equity (ROE), and debt levels. By scrutinizing these factors, investors can gauge whether a company's growth potential is sustainable and whether its stock is worth purchasing.

2. Technical Analysis

While growth investing is primarily rooted in fundamental analysis, some investors also use technical analysis to time their entry and exit points. Technical analysis involves studying stock price charts, trends, and trading volumes to identify patterns and potential price movements. While controversial among investors, technical analysis can provide insights into market sentiment and short-term price movements.

3. Sector and Industry Analysis

Identifying promising sectors and industries can guide growth investors toward companies with the highest growth potential. Emerging technologies, healthcare innovation, and renewable energy are examples of sectors with substantial growth prospects. By researching and understanding macroeconomic trends, investors can position themselves to benefit from larger market dynamics.

4. Growth at a Reasonable Price (GARP)

The GARP strategy seeks a balance between growth and valuation. Investors using this approach focus on companies with strong growth potential that are trading at reasonable valuations. GARP investors avoid overpaying for growth stocks, which can mitigate risks associated with inflated valuations.

Benefits of Growth Investing

Growth investing offers several potential benefits that attract investors seeking significant returns:

1. High Return Potential

The primary allure of growth investing is the potential for substantial returns. Companies experiencing rapid earnings growth can see their stock prices rise exponentially, leading to impressive gains for investors who bought in early.

2. Exposure to Innovation

Growth stocks often emerge from innovative industries and disruptive technologies. By investing in these companies, investors can gain exposure to cutting-edge advancements and breakthroughs, potentially positioning themselves to profit from transformative trends.

3. Long-Term Wealth Accumulation

Investing in companies with sustainable growth potential can lead to long-term wealth accumulation. Holding onto growth stocks as they continue to expand can result in compounding returns, magnifying the initial investment over time.

Risks and Challenges of Growth Investing

While growth investing offers enticing potential rewards, it is not without its fair share of risks and challenges:

1. Volatility

Growth stocks tend to be more volatile than established, dividend-paying companies. Their prices can experience rapid fluctuations due to changes in investor sentiment, market conditions, or company-specific news.

2. Valuation Risk

One of the primary risks associated with growth investing is the potential for overvaluation. Investors may become overly optimistic about a company's growth prospects and bid up its stock price to unsustainable levels. If the company fails to meet overly optimistic expectations, the stock can experience a significant correction.

3. Business Risk

Companies with high growth potential often operate in competitive and dynamic industries. There is a risk that these companies may not be able to maintain their growth trajectory due to increased competition, changing consumer preferences, or unforeseen challenges.

4. Lack of Dividends

Many growth companies reinvest their earnings back into the business to fund expansion. This means they often do not pay dividends to shareholders. While this can lead to potential capital appreciation, it also means investors may not receive regular income from their investments.

Mitigating Risks and Making Informed Decisions

To navigate the risks associated with growth investing, investors can consider the following strategies:

1. Diversification

Diversifying a growth-focused portfolio across different industries, sectors, and geographies can help reduce risk. A diversified portfolio is less likely to be significantly impacted by the underperformance of a single company.

2. Thorough Research

In-depth research is essential before investing in any growth stock. Investigate a company's financials, growth prospects, competitive landscape, and management quality. By making informed decisions, investors can better assess the potential risks and rewards.

3. Long-Term Perspective

Growth investing is inherently a long-term strategy. Investors should be prepared to hold onto their growth stocks through market fluctuations and short-term volatility to reap the benefits of compounding growth over time.

Conclusion

Growth investing offers the potential for impressive returns by identifying and investing in companies with high growth potential. This strategy relies on careful analysis of a company's financial health, growth prospects, and industry dynamics. While the allure of substantial gains is undeniable, growth investing comes with inherent risks, including volatility, overvaluation, and business challenges. Mitigating these risks requires diversification, thorough research, and a long-term perspective. By understanding the principles, strategies, benefits, and risks of growth investing, investors can make informed decisions as they navigate the dynamic landscape of the stock market.

Chapter 10. Psychology of Investing

Introduction

Investing in the stock market can be both exhilarating and nerve-wracking. While the potential for substantial financial gains is alluring, the path to success is riddled with uncertainty and influenced by a complex web of human emotions. Understanding the psychology of investing is crucial for making informed and rational decisions in a volatile market. This chapter delves into the intricate interplay of emotions like greed, fear, and panic and their profound impact on stock investment decisions.

The Emotional Rollercoaster

1. Greed: The Double-Edged Sword

Greed, often portrayed as an insatiable desire for wealth, can significantly influence investment decisions. The prospect of high returns can trigger an overpowering greed that tempts investors to take on excessive risk, neglecting fundamental principles of diversification and risk management. In the pursuit of quick gains, investors might become susceptible to speculative bubbles, investing in overhyped stocks without proper due diligence. Recognizing the signs of greed and practicing disciplined decision-making can mitigate its detrimental effects.

2. Fear: The Paralyzing Agent

Fear is a primal emotion deeply rooted in human psychology, often amplified in the context of investing. The fear of losing money can lead to hesitant decision-making, causing investors to miss out on potentially profitable opportunities. During market downturns, fear can escalate into panic, driving mass sell-offs and exacerbating market volatility. Understanding that fear is a natural response to uncertainty and market fluctuations can help investors maintain a more balanced perspective and prevent knee-jerk reactions.

3. Overcoming Cognitive Biases

Confirmation Bias: Investors tend to seek information that confirms their preexisting beliefs, ignoring data that contradicts their views. This bias can lead to overconfidence in investment decisions and a failure to critically evaluate potential risks.

Loss Aversion: The pain of loss is psychologically more potent than the pleasure of gain. This bias can result in holding onto losing investments for too long, hoping for a rebound, rather than cutting losses and reallocating funds more strategically.

Herd Mentality: Humans have an innate tendency to follow the crowd, especially in uncertain situations. This behavior can lead to the formation of market bubbles or crashes, as individuals make decisions based on the actions of others rather than on objective analysis.

Emotions and Investment Decision-Making

1. The Role of Rationality

While emotions can cloud judgment, it's important to recognize that emotions and rationality are not mutually exclusive. Emotions provide valuable insights into an investor's risk tolerance and psychological biases. Integrating emotions with rational analysis can lead to more balanced investment decisions that align with an individual's financial goals.

2. Setting Realistic Expectations

Managing emotions begins with setting realistic expectations. Understanding that the stock market is inherently volatile can help investors brace for inevitable market fluctuations. Adopting a long-term perspective can mitigate the anxiety induced by short-term market turbulence and provide a more accurate assessment of investment performance.

3. The Importance of a Well-Defined Strategy

A well-defined investment strategy serves as a compass, guiding decisions through market ups and downs. By outlining clear goals, risk tolerance, and exit strategies, investors can avoid impulsive decisions driven by emotions. Regularly reviewing and adjusting the strategy based on changing market conditions ensures a proactive approach to managing investments.

Strategies for Emotionally Intelligent Investing

1. Practicing Mindfulness

Mindfulness involves staying present and aware of one's thoughts and emotions without judgment. Applying mindfulness techniques to investment decisions can help investors recognize emotional triggers and pause before making impulsive choices. This enables more deliberate and rational decision-making.

2. Diversification and Risk Management

Diversification is a fundamental strategy that can counteract the impact of emotional decision-making. Spreading investments across different asset classes and industries reduces the impact of a single investment's poor performance. Implementing risk management techniques, such as setting stop-loss orders, can further protect against emotionally driven losses.

3. Utilizing Technology and Automation

Technology offers tools that can mitigate emotional biases. Robo-advisors, for instance, use algorithms to create and manage diversified portfolios based on an investor's risk profile. Robo-advisors are automated digital platforms that provide algorithm-driven financial planning and investment services, offering personalized and diversified portfolio recommendations based on individual investor goals, risk tolerance, and market conditions, often with lower fees compared to traditional human financial advisors. Automation minimizes the emotional influence on investment decisions, ensuring a disciplined approach to buying and selling assets.

Navigating Market Volatility

1. Education as a Buffer

A well-informed investor is better equipped to handle market volatility. Educating oneself about market dynamics, economic indicators, and historical trends can provide a broader context for interpreting market movements and making rational decisions.

2. Maintaining Perspective

During times of extreme market volatility, maintaining perspective is crucial. Remembering that market fluctuations are a natural part of the investing journey can prevent emotional responses that could lead to poor decisions. A focus on long-term goals helps counteract the impulse to react to short-term market noise.

Conclusion

The psychology of investing is a labyrinth of emotions that can either drive investors toward success or lead them astray. Recognizing the influence of emotions such as greed, fear, and panic is the first step toward developing emotional intelligence in investing. Combining rational analysis with an understanding of these emotions can lead to a more informed and balanced approach to navigating the stock market's unpredictable terrain. By setting realistic expectations, adhering to a well-defined strategy, and embracing emotionally intelligent investing techniques, individuals can strive for better financial outcomes and a more confident journey in the world of stock investments.

Chapter 11. Behavioral Biases

Introduction

In the fast-paced and complex world of the stock market, making informed investment decisions is crucial for achieving financial success. However, despite the availability of data, advanced analysis tools, and expert advice, investors often find themselves influenced by their own emotions and cognitive biases. These behavioral biases can lead to poor investment choices, negatively impacting portfolios and long-term financial goals. In this chapter, we will explore some common cognitive biases that affect stock market investors and discuss strategies to overcome them.

The Role of Behavioral Biases in Investment Decisions

Investing in the stock market is not solely based on cold, rational analysis. Emotions and cognitive biases play a significant role in shaping an investor's decisions. These biases are mental shortcuts that our brains use to make quick judgments and decisions, but they can often lead us astray in complex financial matters.

1. Overconfidence Bias

Overconfidence bias refers to the tendency of investors to believe that their knowledge, skills, and predictions are more accurate than they actually are.

Overconfidence bias can lead investors to underestimate risks and overestimate potential returns. This can result in reckless investment choices and a failure to adequately diversify portfolios. To counteract overconfidence bias, investors should remain humble and recognize the limits of their knowledge. Seeking advice from experts and conducting thorough research can help provide a more balanced perspective.

2. Loss Aversion

Loss aversion is the tendency for investors to feel the pain of losses more intensely than the pleasure of gains.

Loss aversion can lead to "holding on" to losing stocks in the hopes of a rebound, even when evidence suggests that it's unlikely. This reluctance to cut losses can lead to further decline in portfolio value. To combat loss aversion, investors should set clear stop-loss levels before investing and stick to them, regardless of emotional attachment.

3. Confirmation Bias

Confirmation bias refers to the tendency to seek out and give more weight to information that confirms preexisting beliefs.

Investors afflicted by confirmation bias might only pay attention to news and opinions that align with their initial investment decisions, ignoring contrary evidence. This can prevent them from making well-informed adjustments to their portfolio. To counteract confirmation bias, investors should actively seek out diverse perspectives and consider potential downsides before making decisions.

4. Herd Mentality

Herd mentality occurs when investors follow the actions of a larger group, often without fully understanding the rationale behind those actions.

Herd mentality can lead to market bubbles and crashes, as seen during the dot-com bubble (occurred in the late 1990s and early 2000s) and the housing crisis of 2008. To avoid this bias, investors should base their decisions on thorough research and analysis rather than blindly following trends.

5. Anchoring Bias

Anchoring bias is the tendency to rely heavily on the first piece of information encountered when making decisions.

This bias can cause investors to anchor their stock valuations to an initial reference point, whether it's accurate or not. It's essential to consider a range of valuation metrics and constantly update information to avoid being anchored to outdated data.

Overcoming Behavioral Biases in Stock Market Investing

Recognizing these cognitive biases is the first step toward overcoming them. However, acknowledging biases alone might not be enough to prevent their influence on investment decisions. Implementing strategies to mitigate their effects is crucial for making rational and well-informed choices.

1. Develop a Solid Investment Strategy

A well-defined investment strategy can act as a compass, guiding investors through market volatility and emotional turbulence. Determine your risk tolerance, investment goals, and time horizon. This strategy should include guidelines on portfolio diversification, asset allocation, and rebalancing.

2. Set Clear Rules and Stick to Them

Establishing clear rules for buying and selling stocks can help reduce the impact of emotions on investment decisions. For instance, set specific stop-loss levels to limit potential losses and adhere to them regardless of short-term market fluctuations.

3. Practice Contrarian Thinking

Contrarian thinking involves deliberately going against the prevailing market sentiment. While it's essential to stay informed, making decisions solely based on popular opinion can lead to herd mentality and poor outcomes. Consider both bullish and bearish perspectives and be willing to make decisions that go against the crowd when backed by sound analysis.

4. Regularly Review and Update Your Portfolio

To counteract confirmation bias and anchoring bias, commit to regularly reviewing and updating your investment portfolio. Markets are dynamic, and new information can significantly impact the value and potential of your investments. Stay open to adjusting your positions based on changing conditions.

5. Avoid Impulsive Decisions

Emotional reactions often drive impulsive decisions, which can lead to poor investment choices. Before making any trade, take a step back and give yourself time to assess the situation rationally. Avoid making decisions solely based on short-term emotions.

6. Seek Professional Advice

Financial advisors and investment professionals can provide valuable insights and guidance, helping you avoid the pitfalls of behavioral biases. They can provide an objective perspective and keep you accountable to your investment strategy.

Conclusion

The stock market is a challenging arena where cognitive biases can distort rational decision-making and lead to poor investment choices. Recognizing and understanding these biases is essential for any investor aiming to navigate the markets successfully. By implementing strategies to overcome these biases, such as developing a solid investment strategy, setting clear rules, practicing contrarian thinking, and seeking professional advice, investors can make more rational and informed decisions that align with their long-term financial goals. Remember, the path to successful investing requires not only understanding the market but also mastering the psychology behind it.

Chapter 12. Emotional Intelligence in Investing

Introduction

In the fast-paced world of stock market investing, where decisions are made in seconds and fortunes can be won or lost in a blink of an eye, emotional intelligence stands as a crucial yet often underestimated factor. In this chapter, we delve into the significance of emotional intelligence in the context of investing, exploring how its development can assist investors in managing their emotions and making rational decisions that drive success in the stock market.

Understanding Emotional Intelligence

Emotional intelligence, often referred to as EQ, is the ability to recognize, understand, manage, and effectively use our own emotions as well as those of others. It encompasses a range of skills, including self-awareness, self-regulation, empathy, and social skills. While emotional intelligence is often associated with personal relationships and leadership, its relevance extends far beyond those realms. In the context of investing, emotional intelligence plays a pivotal role in shaping an investor's decision-making process.

The Emotional Roller Coaster of the Stock Market

Investing in the stock market can be a roller coaster ride of emotions. Market fluctuations, economic news, and unexpected events can trigger a range of emotions, from euphoria to panic. Emotional responses, if left unchecked, can lead to impulsive and irrational decisions that undermine investment strategies.

The Impact of Fear and Greed

Fear and greed are two powerful emotions that frequently drive investors' decisions. Fear can lead to a rush to sell during market downturns, even when it might be more prudent to hold onto assets. Greed, on the other hand, can result in chasing speculative investments without due diligence. Emotional intelligence helps investors recognize these emotions and respond to them in a more measured and rational manner.

Developing Emotional Intelligence for Investors

Investors can actively cultivate emotional intelligence to enhance their decision-making capabilities in the stock market. Here are some strategies to consider.

1. Self-Awareness: Recognizing Emotions

Investors must first become aware of their emotional responses. Keeping a trading journal to track emotions during various market events can help identify patterns of behavior. Recognizing when fear or greed is influencing decisions is the first step toward managing them.

2. Self-Regulation: Managing Emotional Responses

Once emotions are recognized, investors can work on regulating their responses. Techniques such as mindfulness meditation, deep breathing exercises, and taking breaks during volatile trading periods can help investors maintain a sense of calm and avoid impulsive actions.

3. Empathy: Understanding Market Sentiment

Empathy involves understanding the emotions of others. In investing, this means comprehending market sentiment and how it can affect stock prices. Developing an empathetic understanding of the collective emotions driving market trends can help investors make more informed decisions.

4. Social Skills: Collaborative Decision-Making

Investors often operate in social environments, whether it's within a team or alongside financial advisors. Effective communication and collaboration skills are vital for successful decision-making. Emotional intelligence enhances an investor's ability to communicate ideas, listen to others, and work collaboratively toward common goals.

The Rational Edge

Emotional intelligence provides investors with a rational edge by helping them navigate the complexities of the stock market with a clear and composed mindset.

1. Countering Cognitive Biases

Cognitive biases, such as confirmation bias and herd mentality, can cloud judgment and lead to poor investment choices. Emotional intelligence enables investors to recognize these biases and counteract them, ensuring decisions are based on well-rounded information rather than emotional inclinations.

2. Long-Term Perspective

Investing with emotional intelligence encourages a long-term perspective. Emotional investors often jump in and out of positions based on short-term market fluctuations. Those with developed emotional intelligence are more likely to stick to a well-thought-out investment strategy, ignoring short-term noise.

3. Risk Management

Risk management is an integral part of successful investing. Emotional intelligence allows investors to assess risks objectively, rather than being swayed by emotional responses. This leads to more accurate risk evaluations and a better understanding of potential rewards.

Real-Life Success Stories

Numerous successful investors credit their emotional intelligence for their achievements in the stock market. Warren Buffett, often considered one of the greatest investors of all time, is known for his ability to remain calm during market turmoil and make rational decisions. His emotional intelligence, combined with his deep analytical skills, has been a cornerstone of his investment strategy.

Conclusion

Emotional intelligence is a valuable asset in the world of stock market investing. Developing emotional intelligence empowers investors to manage their emotions, make rational decisions, and achieve long-term success. By cultivating self-awareness, practicing self-regulation, honing empathy, and fostering social skills, investors can gain a competitive edge and navigate the unpredictable waters of the stock market with confidence. As the financial landscape continues to evolve, emotional intelligence remains a timeless tool that stands as a pillar of rational decision-making for investors of all levels.

Chapter 13. Diversification Strategies

Introduction

Investing in the stock market can be both thrilling and nerve-wracking. The potential for substantial gains is alluring, but the inherent volatility and uncertainty can also lead to sleepless nights. This is where the concept of diversification comes into play. Diversification, often touted as the golden rule of investing, is a strategy that aims to manage risk and enhance overall portfolio stability by spreading investments across different assets. In this chapter, we will delve into the importance of diversification strategies in the stock market and explore various techniques to implement them effectively.

Understanding the Importance of Diversification

1. The Risk-Return Tradeoff

When it comes to investing, risk and return are intrinsically linked. The potential for higher returns usually comes with a higher level of risk. In the world of stocks, this risk can be amplified due to factors such as market sentiment, economic fluctuations, industry-specific events, and company performance. Diversification acknowledges this tradeoff and seeks to strike a balance between maximizing returns and minimizing risk.

2. Single-Stock Exposure: A Recipe for Disaster

Imagine placing all your eggs in one basket – if that basket falls, you're left with nothing. The same principle applies to investing. Relying heavily on a single stock can be a dangerous endeavor. Even the most promising companies can face unforeseen challenges, leading to significant drops in stock value. Diversification helps avoid the catastrophic impact of such events by reducing exposure to a single asset.

3. Portfolio Volatility Reduction

Volatility is the hallmark of the stock market. Prices can swing dramatically in a short period. Diversification acts as a stabilizer, diluting the impact of sharp declines in one asset with the potential gains in another. A well-diversified portfolio tends to experience less extreme fluctuations, providing investors with a smoother journey through the tumultuous waters of the stock market.

Principles of Diversification

1. Spreading Across Asset Classes

Effective diversification goes beyond just investing in a handful of stocks. It involves spreading investments across different asset classes, such as stocks, bonds, real estate, and commodities. Each asset class reacts differently to market conditions, so a downturn in one area may be offset by stability or growth in another. By diversifying across asset classes, investors can reduce the overall risk exposure of their portfolio.

2. Embracing Industry and Sector Diversity

Within the realm of stocks, diversification extends to various industries and sectors. Different sectors perform differently based on economic trends, technological advancements, and consumer behavior. Allocating investments across sectors like technology, healthcare, finance, and energy ensures that the performance of one sector doesn't overly impact the entire portfolio.

3. Geographic Diversification: Going Global

In today's interconnected world, geographic diversification has gained prominence. Investing solely in one country exposes your portfolio to the risks and rewards of that nation's economy. By including international stocks, you can mitigate the impact of country-specific events and tap into the growth potential of different markets.

Strategies for Effective Diversification

1. The Rule of Thumb: The 60/40 Split

One widely used diversification strategy is the 60/40 split. This entails allocating 60% of the portfolio to stocks and 40% to bonds. Stocks offer growth potential, while bonds provide stability and income. This combination balances the risk-reward equation, especially for investors with a lower risk tolerance.

2. Modern Portfolio Theory and the Efficient Frontier

Modern Portfolio Theory (MPT) revolutionized diversification by introducing the concept of the efficient frontier. MPT suggests that by selecting a mix of assets with varying risk and return profiles, investors can create portfolios that maximize return for a given level of risk or minimize risk for a given level of return. This mathematical approach guides investors to find the optimal balance based on their risk preferences.

3. Exchange-Traded Funds (ETFs) and Mutual Funds

For those seeking diversification without the hassle of handpicking individual stocks and bonds, exchange-traded funds (ETFs) and mutual funds offer a convenient solution. These investment vehicles pool money from multiple investors to buy a diversified collection of assets. ETFs and mutual funds can provide exposure to different sectors, industries, and even geographic regions in a single investment.

4. Rebalancing: Maintaining the Balance

Diversification isn't a one-time task; it requires ongoing maintenance. As assets perform differently over time, the original allocation can shift, impacting the risk profile of the portfolio. Rebalancing involves periodically readjusting the portfolio to its original allocation. This ensures that the benefits of diversification remain intact and that the portfolio remains aligned with the investor's risk tolerance.

Conclusion

In the unpredictable realm of the stock market, diversification emerges as a powerful tool for investors seeking stability and risk mitigation. By spreading investments across different asset classes, sectors, and geographic regions, diversification minimizes the impact of adverse events and enhances the potential for consistent returns. Whether following the principles of the 60/40 split, leveraging Modern Portfolio Theory, or opting for ETFs and mutual funds, investors have an array of strategies to implement effective diversification.

Remember, the goal of diversification is not to eliminate risk entirely, but to manage and control it. Every investment decision carries some level of risk, but through thoughtful diversification, investors can navigate the unpredictable waters of the stock market with greater confidence and resilience. As the investment landscape continues to evolve, embracing diversification as a core principle remains a timeless strategy for building a robust and enduring portfolio.

Chapter 14. Asset Allocation

Introduction

In the dynamic world of investing, one of the key strategies that can significantly impact your portfolio's performance is asset allocation. Asset allocation is the process of dividing your investment capital among different asset classes, such as stocks, bonds, and alternative investments, with the goal of achieving a balance between risk and reward. This chapter delves into the importance of asset allocation and provides insights into how to effectively allocate your investments to navigate the complex landscape of the stock market.

Understanding Asset Allocation: Balancing Risk and Reward

At the heart of successful investing lies the principle of diversification, and asset allocation is a prime example of this principle in action. The goal of asset allocation is to create a diversified portfolio that mitigates risk and maximizes returns over time. Different asset classes have varying risk-return profiles, and by allocating your investments across them, you can harness the benefits of each class while reducing exposure to their respective drawbacks.

The Core Asset Classes: Stocks, Bonds, and Alternative Investments

1. Stocks: The Engine of Growth

Stocks, also known as equities, represent ownership in a company. They are renowned for their potential to offer substantial capital appreciation over the long term. However, this growth potential comes with higher volatility and risk. Stocks are a core component of most investment portfolios, and the proportion allocated to them often depends on the investor's risk tolerance and investment horizon.

2. Bonds: Stability and Income

Bonds are fixed-income securities issued by governments and corporations. They provide regular interest payments (coupon payments) to investors and return the principal amount at maturity. Bonds are generally considered less risky than stocks, making them a popular choice for investors seeking stability and consistent income. The allocation to bonds in a portfolio can provide a cushion during market downturns and act as a counterbalance to the potential volatility of stocks.

3. Alternative Investments: Expanding Horizons

Alternative investments encompass a wide range of assets beyond traditional stocks and bonds. Examples include real estate, commodities, hedge funds, private equity, and cryptocurrencies. These investments often have unique risk-return profiles and low correlation with traditional asset classes. Including a small portion of alternative investments in your portfolio can enhance diversification and potentially improve risk-adjusted returns.

Determining Your Asset Allocation Strategy

1. Risk Tolerance and Investment Goals

Your risk tolerance and investment goals are foundational in shaping your asset allocation strategy. Risk tolerance refers to your ability and willingness to withstand market fluctuations. Conservative investors might lean towards a higher allocation to bonds, while aggressive investors might favor a larger portion of stocks. Additionally, your investment goals, whether they involve wealth preservation, growth, or income generation, play a significant role in determining the mix of assets in your portfolio.

2. Time Horizon

The time horizon, or the duration you plan to hold your investments, also impacts your asset allocation. Longer investment horizons can tolerate more volatility, potentially allowing for a higher allocation to growth-oriented assets like stocks. Shorter horizons might necessitate a more conservative approach to preserve capital and reduce the impact of market downturns.

3. Market Conditions

Market conditions can influence the attractiveness of various asset classes. During bullish periods, stocks might be on an upswing, while during economic downturns, bonds could offer stability. Staying attuned to market trends and adjusting your asset allocation periodically can optimize your portfolio's performance and risk exposure.

Strategies for Asset Allocation

1. Strategic Asset Allocation

Strategic asset allocation involves creating a fixed allocation plan based on your risk tolerance and investment goals. This strategy emphasizes long-term stability and involves periodic rebalancing to maintain the desired asset allocation. Rebalancing ensures that the proportions of different asset classes remain consistent, which can help investors buy low and sell high over time.

2. Tactical Asset Allocation

Tactical asset allocation involves making short-term adjustments to your portfolio's allocation based on your outlook for specific asset classes or market conditions. This approach requires a deeper understanding of market trends and the ability to seize opportunities as they arise. While potentially rewarding, tactical asset allocation can also increase transaction costs and market timing risks.

3. Dynamic Asset Allocation

Dynamic asset allocation integrates elements of both strategic and tactical approaches. It involves periodically adjusting your portfolio based on changes in your investment goals, risk tolerance, and market conditions. This flexibility allows you to respond to evolving circumstances while maintaining a core strategic framework.

Monitoring and Rebalancing

1. The Importance of Rebalancing

Over time, as the performance of different asset classes diverges, your portfolio's original asset allocation can become skewed. Rebalancing involves selling portions of outperforming assets and reinvesting in underperforming ones to restore the desired balance. This process enforces the principle of "buying low and selling high" and prevents your portfolio from becoming overly concentrated in a single asset class.

2. Rebalancing Frequencies

The frequency of rebalancing depends on your investment strategy and the level of market volatility. Some investors rebalance annually, while others opt for quarterly or even more frequent intervals. Modern portfolio management tools and robo-advisors can assist in automating the rebalancing process, ensuring that your portfolio remains aligned with your goals.

Conclusion

Asset allocation is a cornerstone of successful investing in the stock market. By thoughtfully distributing your investments across various asset classes, you can achieve a balance between risk and reward, enhancing your chances of meeting your financial goals. Understanding your risk tolerance, investment horizon, and market conditions are pivotal in determining your asset allocation strategy. Whether you choose a strategic, tactical, or dynamic approach, regular monitoring and rebalancing are key to maintaining the integrity of your portfolio. As you navigate the complex world of investing, remember that a well-structured asset allocation strategy can serve as your guiding compass towards building a resilient and prosperous investment portfolio.

Chapter 15. Portfolio Rebalancing

Introduction

In the dynamic world of stock market investing, maintaining a diversified and well-structured portfolio is essential to achieving long-term financial goals. While constructing a portfolio involves careful consideration of risk tolerance, investment objectives, and time horizon, the journey doesn't end once the initial allocation is made. Portfolio rebalancing, a critical aspect of investment management, ensures that the portfolio remains aligned with the investor's desired risk and return levels over time. In this chapter, we delve into the concept of portfolio rebalancing, exploring its significance, strategies, and best practices.

The Significance of Portfolio Rebalancing

1. A Dynamic Investment Landscape

The stock market is characterized by volatility, economic fluctuations, and changing market trends. Consequently, the initial asset allocation of a portfolio can deviatc significantly over time, leading to a mismatch between an investor's risk preferences and their actual exposure to risk. Portfolio rebalancing aims to address this disparity and maintain the desired risk and return profile.

2. Balancing Risk and Return

The fundamental principle behind portfolio rebalancing is to strike a balance between risk and return. As certain asset classes outperform others, the portfolio's composition can shift, potentially exposing the investor to greater risk or lower returns than intended. By regularly reviewing and adjusting the portfolio, investors can ensure that they are not overexposed to high-risk assets during market upswings or overly conservative during market downturns.

3. The Behavioral Aspect

Human psychology can play a significant role in investment decisions. Investors may become emotionally attached to certain investments that have performed well or be reluctant to sell underperforming assets. This emotional bias can lead to an unbalanced portfolio. Rebalancing provides a systematic approach that removes emotions from the equation, fostering disciplined decision-making.

When to Rebalance: Timing and Triggers

1. Time-Based Rebalancing

One common approach to portfolio rebalancing is time-based, where the investor allocates specific intervals for assessment and adjustment. For example, an investor might choose to rebalance their portfolio annually or semi-annually. While this method ensures a regular review of the portfolio's composition, it might not align perfectly with market conditions.

2. Threshold-Based Rebalancing

Threshold-based rebalancing involves setting predefined percentage thresholds for each asset class within the portfolio. When the actual allocation deviates from these thresholds, a rebalancing action is triggered. This approach ensures that rebalancing occurs when deviations are significant enough to impact the overall risk and return profile.

3. Calendar vs. Percentage: Finding the Right Balance

Deciding between time-based and threshold-based rebalancing depends on individual preferences and market conditions. A calendar-based approach offers simplicity and consistency, while a percentage-based approach allows for more flexibility in response to market movements. Finding the right balance between the two is crucial to optimizing the rebalancing process.

How to Rebalance: Strategies and Considerations

1. Selling High, Buying Low

The essence of portfolio rebalancing lies in the principle of selling overperforming assets and buying underperforming ones. This counterintuitive strategy encourages investors to take profits when assets are doing well and acquire assets that are currently undervalued. This approach aligns with the age-old investment adage: "Buy low, sell high."

2. Minimizing Transaction Costs and Taxes

Rebalancing can incur transaction costs, such as brokerage fees and bid-ask spreads. Additionally, capital gains taxes may apply to profits realized from selling appreciated assets. To mitigate these costs, investors should consider tax-efficient strategies, such as tax-loss harvesting, and consolidate rebalancing actions to minimize trading expenses.

3. Considering Market Trends and Economic Conditions

Effective portfolio rebalancing requires a comprehensive understanding of market trends and economic conditions.

It's essential to evaluate whether shifts in asset class performance are temporary or indicative of a longer-term trend. In some cases, a deviation from the target allocation might be justified if supported by robust market analysis.

4. Reassessing Risk Tolerance and Investment Goals

Investors' risk tolerance and financial goals may evolve over time due to life events, changing priorities, or market experiences. Periodic rebalancing offers an opportunity to reassess these factors and adjust the portfolio's composition accordingly. A well-aligned portfolio not only reflects an investor's risk appetite but also aligns with their broader financial aspirations.

Best Practices for Portfolio Rebalancing

1. Set Clear Goals and Parameters

Before embarking on the rebalancing journey, investors should establish clear goals and parameters. Determine the target asset allocation, preferred rebalancing method, and specific triggers for adjustments. These guidelines provide a roadmap for effective rebalancing decisions.

2. Utilize Automation Tools

Technology has simplified the rebalancing process through the use of automation tools and robo-advisors. These platforms can automatically analyze portfolio deviations, calculate required adjustments, and execute trades, all while minimizing emotional biases and human errors.

3. Stay Disciplined in Volatile Markets

Market volatility can trigger knee-jerk reactions, tempting investors to deviate from their rebalancing strategy. However, it's crucial to stay disciplined and adhere to the established plan. Emotional decision-making can disrupt the intended risk-return balance and hinder long-term performance.

4. Seek Professional Guidance

For investors seeking personalized advice or lacking the time and expertise for in-depth portfolio management, consulting with financial advisors is a prudent step. Financial professionals can tailor rebalancing strategies to individual circumstances and provide insights into navigating complex market dynamics.

Conclusion

Portfolio rebalancing is a cornerstone of effective investment management. By systematically adjusting a portfolio's composition over time, investors can ensure that their risk and return objectives remain aligned, even in the face of shifting market conditions. While the rebalancing process requires careful consideration and strategic thinking, its benefits are clear: reduced risk exposure, optimized returns, and the cultivation of disciplined investment behavior. As investors continue their journey in the stock market, embracing portfolio rebalancing as a core practice will undoubtedly contribute to their long-term financial success.

Chapter 16. Long-Term Investing

Introduction

In the fast-paced world of stock investing, the allure of quick gains often takes center stage. However, for those who truly understand the power of compounding and the value of patience, long-term investing emerges as a tried-and-true strategy for accumulating significant wealth over time. In this chapter, we will delve into the world of long-term investing, exploring its benefits, principles, and practical tips for successful wealth accumulation in the stock market.

Benefits of Long-Term Investing

1. Harnessing the Power of Compounding

At the heart of long-term investing lies the concept of compounding. Compounding is the snowball effect that occurs when your investments generate returns, and those returns, in turn, generate even more returns. Over time, compounding can significantly magnify your initial investments, leading to exponential growth. The key to making compounding work in your favor is time. The longer your money remains invested, the greater the compounding effect. By staying invested for the long term, you allow your investments to ride out the inevitable market fluctuations and benefit from the magic of compounding.

2. Embracing the Ups and Downs of the Market

The stock market is known for its volatility, with prices often swinging wildly in response to economic, political, and global events. Long-term investors understand that short-term fluctuations are a natural part of the market's cycle. By adopting a patient approach, you can weather these ups and downs without succumbing to panic selling or impulsive decision-making. Instead of chasing short-term gains, you focus on the bigger picture and allow your investments to grow over time.

3. Reducing Transaction Costs and Taxes

Frequent buying and selling of stocks can lead to substantial transaction costs and tax implications. Long-term investors benefit from reduced transaction expenses as they make fewer trades. Additionally, many countries offer tax incentives for holding investments for the long term, allowing investors to retain more of their gains. By minimizing turnover in your portfolio, you not only save on costs but also create a tax-efficient strategy for building wealth.

Principles of Long-Term Investing

1. Research and Select Quality Investments

Successful long-term investing starts with thorough research and due diligence. Identify companies with strong fundamentals, a history of consistent earnings growth, and a competitive advantage in their industry. Diversification is also key; spreading your investments across different sectors and industries can help mitigate risks associated with individual stock volatility.

2. Patience is Your Greatest Asset

Patience is the cornerstone of long-term investing. Resist the urge to constantly monitor your investments and make knee-jerk reactions to short-term market movements. Instead, focus on your investment thesis and the long-term prospects of the companies you've invested in. The stock market's performance over years, not days or months, is what truly matters.

3. Dollar-Cost Averaging

Dollar-cost averaging involves investing a fixed amount of money at regular intervals, regardless of market conditions. This strategy helps reduce the impact of market volatility on your portfolio. When prices are high, you buy fewer shares, and when prices are low, you buy more shares. Over time, this approach can lead to a lower average cost per share and smoother returns.

4. Reinvest Dividends

Dividend-paying stocks can be valuable assets for long-term investors. Reinvesting dividends allows you to harness the power of compounding even further. By using dividend payouts to purchase additional shares of the same stock, you increase your ownership stake and potential for future returns.

Practical Tips for Successful Long-Term Investing

1. Set Clear Goals and a Long-Term Horizon

Before embarking on your long-term investing journey, define your financial goals. Whether it's funding your children's education, building a retirement nest egg, or achieving financial independence, having clear objectives will guide your investment decisions. Additionally, establish a long-term time horizon, ideally spanning decades. This perspective will help you stay focused on the bigger picture and resist short-term distractions.

2. Maintain a Balanced Portfolio

While long-term investing emphasizes patience, it doesn't mean you should ignore your portfolio altogether. Regularly review your holdings and make adjustments as needed to maintain a balanced allocation. As you progress toward your goals, your risk tolerance and financial situation may change, warranting a reevaluation of your investment mix.

3. Stay Informed but Avoid Overreacting

Staying informed about market trends and economic developments is essential, but it's equally important to avoid overreacting to every piece of news. Remember that the stock market is influenced by a multitude of factors, and short-term fluctuations are part of the game. Make informed decisions based on your research and investment thesis rather than succumbing to market noise.

4. Stick to Your Strategy

In moments of market turmoil, it's easy to second-guess your investment strategy. However, sticking to your well-researched plan is crucial. Emotional decision-making can lead to missed opportunities or unnecessary losses. Remind yourself of your long-term goals and the principles of long-term investing to stay the course.

Conclusion

Long-term investing is a journey that requires patience, discipline, and a steadfast commitment to your financial goals. By harnessing the power of compounding, embracing market volatility, and adhering to sound investment principles, you can build significant wealth over time. Remember that success in the stock market is not measured by quick gains but by the steady accumulation of wealth that sustains your financial aspirations. As you navigate the intricate world of investing, keep the wisdom of long-term strategies close to heart, and let time work its magic on your path to prosperity.

Chapter 17. Contrarian Investing

Introduction

In the ever-evolving landscape of the stock market, there's a widely followed adage: "Buy low, sell high." While it may seem like common sense, the reality of practicing this philosophy is often overshadowed by the emotional rollercoaster of market sentiment. This is where contrarian investing comes into play. Contrarian investing is not just a strategy; it's a mindset that challenges conventional wisdom by advocating the purchase of stocks that are currently out of favor. In this chapter, we'll delve into the concept of contrarian investing, its rationale, benefits, risks, and how to effectively implement this strategy in your investment journey.

Understanding Contrarian Investing

Contrarian investing is grounded in the belief that the market tends to overreact to news, events, and trends, causing stock prices to deviate from their intrinsic values. This phenomenon often results in the undervaluation or overvaluation of stocks. Contrarian investors seek to capitalize on these mispricings by going against the crowd and investing in stocks that others are shying away from. This strategy requires a strong belief in the concept of mean reversion, where assets that have experienced significant price movements tend to eventually revert to their historical average.

The Psychology of Market Sentiment

Contrarian investing goes hand in hand with understanding the psychology of market sentiment. Markets are driven by fear and greed, and these emotions can lead to market extremes. When news is positive and stocks are soaring, investors become euphoric and flock to buy. Conversely, during times of economic uncertainty or negative news, panic ensues, leading to widespread selling. Contrarian investors recognize that these emotions can create opportunities to enter or exit positions at advantageous prices.

Rationale Behind Contrarian Investing

1. Buy Low, Sell High: The Essence of Contrarianism

The central tenet of contrarian investing is the idea of buying low and selling high. This seems obvious, but in practice, it requires the discipline to act against prevailing sentiments. Contrarian investors take advantage of undervalued stocks that are trading below their intrinsic value, offering a margin of safety. This safety net provides a buffer against potential downturns and increases the potential for substantial gains when the market eventually corrects itself.

2. Avoiding the Herd Mentality

Herd mentality can lead to asset bubbles and market crashes. Contrarian investors recognize the danger of following the crowd blindly and strive to avoid being swept up in market euphoria or panic. By going against the herd, they position themselves to take advantage of the market's irrational behavior, purchasing assets when they are unfairly beaten down and selling when they become overinflated.

Benefits and Risks of Contrarian Investing

Benefits

1. Value Discovery

Contrarian investors uncover hidden gems that others have overlooked due to short-term volatility or negative sentiment. By conducting thorough research and analysis, they identify stocks with solid fundamentals that are likely to rebound in the long run.

2. Lower Entry Prices

Investing when stocks are out of favor allows contrarian investors to enter positions at lower prices. This reduces the risk of buying at the peak of a market bubble and increases the potential for higher returns when the market eventually corrects itself.

3. Potential for Higher Returns

When the market sentiment shifts and stocks recover, contrarian investors can experience significant gains as the stocks they purchased at lower prices appreciate in value. The disconnect between the stock's current price and its true value creates a profit opportunity.

Risks

1. Value Trap

Not all undervalued stocks are poised for recovery. Some may be undervalued for valid reasons, such as poor management, declining industries, or unsustainable business models. Contrarian investors must be cautious not to fall into the trap of buying stocks that are fundamentally flawed and unlikely to rebound.

2. Timing Challenges

Timing the market is a complex endeavor, and contrarian investing is no exception. Stocks can remain undervalued for extended periods, and it takes patience to wait for the market sentiment to shift. Investors need to be prepared for potential short-term losses before reaping long-term gains.

3. Emotional Resilience

Contrarian investing can be emotionally taxing. Watching your investments decline while the broader market is thriving requires a strong conviction in your analysis and a steady hand to avoid panic selling.

Implementing a Contrarian Investing Strategy

1. Thorough Research

Before investing in any out-of-favor stock, thorough research is essential. Analyze the company's financials, competitive positioning, industry trends, and management quality. Assess whether the stock's current low valuation is justified by its underlying fundamentals.

2. Long-Term Perspective

Contrarian investing is not a short-term game. It requires a long-term perspective and the willingness to hold onto undervalued stocks even as short-term fluctuations occur. Patience is a virtue in this strategy.

3. Diversification

Diversification is a fundamental principle of investing, and contrarian investors should adhere to it as well. Spreading investments across different sectors and industries reduces the impact of poor performance in any single stock on your overall portfolio.

4. Contrarian ≠ Blind Contrary

Being a contrarian doesn't mean ignoring market trends altogether. Sometimes, there's a valid reason why a stock is underperforming. Distinguish between stocks with temporary issues that are likely to rebound and those facing insurmountable challenges.

5. Staying Updated

Keep a close watch on news, market trends, and the company's performance even after investing. Contrarian investing requires active monitoring to determine whether the initial investment thesis is playing out as expected.

The Bottom Line

Contrarian investing is not for the faint of heart, but for those willing to embrace its principles, it can yield substantial rewards. By seeking opportunities where others see pitfalls and approaching the market with a rational and long-term perspective, contrarian investors have the potential to profit from market inefficiencies. Remember, the road less traveled may be fraught with uncertainties, but it can lead to uncharted territory and untapped potential, making it a valuable strategy to consider in your investment journey.

Chapter 18. Learning from Mistakes

Introduction

Investing in the stock market can be both exhilarating and intimidating. The allure of significant gains often overshadows the inherent risks that accompany such ventures. Many investors find themselves caught in the throes of the market's ups and downs, making both wise decisions and unfortunate blunders. This chapter delves into the realm of real-life case studies to shed light on the valuable lessons that emerge from stock investment successes and failures. By dissecting these stories, we can glean insights into the intricacies of the stock market and refine our strategies for informed decision-making.

The Dichotomy of Success and Failure

The journey of a stock market investor is marked by a series of choices, some yielding substantial returns and others leading to losses. These fluctuations can often be attributed to the complex interplay of various factors, including market trends, company performance, and broader economic conditions. To truly grasp the nuances of investing, let's explore both sides of the coin through real-life case studies.

Case Study 1: Triumph in the Face of Adversity - Amazon

Amazon, the e-commerce giant founded by Jeff Bezos, has become a symbol of remarkable success. However, this success was not without its initial setbacks and controversies. In the late 1990s, during the dot-com bubble,

Amazon's stock price plummeted along with numerous other tech companies. Investors who panicked and sold their shares faced substantial losses. Those who stayed the course, however, reaped the rewards of Amazon's eventual rise to dominance.

Lessons Learned

Long-Term Vision: Amazon's story underscores the importance of adopting a long-term perspective. Short-term fluctuations should not deter investors from believing in a company's potential to innovate and grow over time.

Resilience in Adversity: Volatile market conditions are par for the course. Investors who weather the storm and remain steadfast in their convictions are more likely to realize substantial gains.

Case Study 2: The Pitfall of Overconfidence - Enron

The case of Enron, once a seemingly invincible energy company, serves as a cautionary tale for investors. In the early 2000s, Enron's stock was soaring, attracting investors with promises of unrivaled profits. However, the company's fraudulent accounting practices and deceptive financial reporting came to light, leading to its eventual bankruptcy and the loss of billions for investors.

Lessons Learned

Due Diligence: Blindly following the hype without conducting thorough research can lead to disaster. Investors should scrutinize a company's financial statements, leadership, and overall business model before committing funds.

Transparency and Ethics: Enron's downfall highlights the significance of ethical business practices and transparent financial reporting. Investors should prioritize companies with integrity and open communication.

Extracting Wisdom from Failure

While failures offer invaluable lessons, they also underscore the importance of heeding early warning signs and avoiding common pitfalls. Let's explore more real-life case studies to deepen our understanding.

Case Study 3: Navigating the Tech Bubble - Pets.com

The late 1990s saw a surge in tech companies entering the stock market, many of which were valued beyond their actual worth. Pets.com, an online pet supply retailer, exemplified this trend. The company went public and gained significant attention, but it struggled to turn a profit. Ultimately, Pets.com became one of the most infamous casualties of the dot-com bubble.

Lessons Learned

Value Proposition: Investors must critically assess a company's ability to generate revenue and provide value to customers. A strong concept or idea is not enough if the business model is not viable.

Sustainability Over Hype: Avoid investing solely based on market trends or hype. Companies with a clear path to profitability and sustainable growth are better choices in the long run.

Case Study 4: Beyond the Hype - Snapchat

Snapchat, the multimedia messaging app, had a highly anticipated initial public offering (IPO) in 2017. While its user base grew rapidly, concerns arose about its ability to monetize its platform. After an initial surge, the stock price began to decline, causing losses for investors who had bought in during the early stages.

Lessons Learned

Profitability Matters: A company's ability to convert its user base into revenue is crucial. Investors should be cautious if a company's growth is not matched by a clear and effective monetization strategy.

Evaluating Future Potential: Even if a company is popular among a younger demographic, investors should evaluate whether its offerings have broader appeal and long-term sustainability.

Embracing Success and Its Blueprint

As investors analyze mistakes, they must also study the pathways to triumph. Real-life examples of stock investment successes can provide valuable insights into crafting effective investment strategies.

Case Study 5: The Apple Resurgence

In the late 1990s, Apple was struggling, and its stock price reflected the company's uncertain future. However, the return of Steve Jobs and his visionary leadership marked a turning point. The introduction of groundbreaking products like the iPod, iPhone, and iPad propelled Apple to new heights, making it one of the most valuable companies globally.

Lessons Learned

Leadership Matters: A strong and visionary leadership team can steer a company through challenges and lead it to innovative breakthroughs.

Adaptation and Innovation: Companies that continually innovate and adapt to changing market landscapes are more likely to remain relevant and thrive.

Case Study 6: Netflix's Evolution

Netflix's transformation from a DVD rental service to a streaming media powerhouse demonstrates the importance of strategic evolution. As the market shifted towards digital streaming, Netflix embraced the change and invested heavily in original content. This strategic shift paid off, and the company's stock price surged.

Lessons Learned

Flexibility and Adaptability: Investors should favor companies that can pivot their strategies to align with industry trends and consumer preferences.

Anticipating Market Shifts: Recognizing emerging trends and positioning investments accordingly can yield significant rewards.

Conclusion

In the realm of stock market investments, both successes and failures offer invaluable lessons. Real-life case studies illustrate the importance of factors such as long-term vision, due diligence, value proposition, sustainable growth, and strategic adaptation. Learning from past mistakes can be the key to making informed decisions and achieving success in the complex and ever-changing landscape of the stock market. By extracting wisdom from both triumphs and pitfalls, investors can refine their strategies and navigate the stock market with increased confidence.

Dive into the world of stock market investing with "Investment Guide for the Stock Market". This comprehensive book equips both novice and experienced investors with essential knowledge and strategies. The book begins with an insightful introduction to the stock market, followed by a thorough comparison between investment and speculation. Delving into key concepts, readers will gain a strong understanding of market indices, cycles, and trends.

The intricate relationship between risk and returns is explored, alongside in-depth examinations of fundamental and technical analysis. From the principles of value and growth investing to the psychology and behavioral biases affecting decisions, this guide offers a holistic view. It also covers diversification, asset allocation, portfolio rebalancing, and the merits of long-term and contrarian investing. Real-world case studies provide practical insights for readers to learn from both triumphs and setbacks. Your journey to mastering stock market investing starts here.

ABOUT THE AUTHOR

Mr. C. P. Kumar is a retired Scientist 'G' from National Institute of Hydrology, Roorkee, Uttarakhand, India. He is also a Reiki Healer and Chakra Balancing practitioner (with pendulum dowsing) and offers Emotional Freedom Technique (EFT) to help individuals with emotional issues. Mr. Kumar has authored many books on technical, spiritual, and social topics.

For further details, you may visit his webpage
https://www.angelfire.com/nh/cpkumar/virgo.html

www.ingramcontent.com/pod-product-compliance
Lightning Source LLC
LaVergne TN
LVHW022112200926
848481LV00003B/1157
* 9 7 9 8 2 2 3 1 3 3 5 4 4 *